Chicks on the Farm

Written by Michèle Dufresne

PIONEER VALLEY EDUCATIONAL PRESS, INC.

Peck! Peck! Peck!
Look! Can you see
a crack in the **egg**?

Look at the ball of fluff.

It is a **chick**!

Chicks are baby chickens. They hatch from eggs after 21 days. Chicks grow very quickly and will double in size in two weeks.

The chicks run
to get a snack.
Peck! Peck! Peck!

Chicks eat grains like corn and wheat. Farmers often give them chick starter feed to help them grow.

The chicks can see a sack. The chicks pick up bits of **corn.** Peck! Peck! Peck!

Flap! Flap! Flap!

Hop! Hop! Hop!

The chicks will go back to the **brooder** to rest.

A brooder is an enclosure that farmers use for chicks when they are very small. The brooder keeps the chicks warm.

Oh no!

Look out for the fox!

Quick, chicks!

Run back to the pen!

Chicks have many predators, like foxes and hawks. Farmers build fences and coops to keep them safe.

Look at the duck.

It can swim.

Can a chick swim? No!

Unlike ducks, chicks cannot swim. Chickens don't have waterproof feathers and can drown in deep water.

The chicks get big. They flap and peck and run. They go back to the **coop** at dusk.

In just six to eight weeks, chicks grow feathers and start to look like hens or roosters. At night, they return to the coop to sleep.

glossary

egg

chick

corn

brooder

coop